Previous Publications:

Born, Black Stone Press, 1975

Handbook of Ornament, Black Stone Press, 1979

The Gospel of Mary, Woodley Press, 1997

god won't overlook us, Penthe Press, 2001

Abundance, 219 Press, 2004

Voice Over, Blue Cedar Press, 2012

And So it Goes, Blue Cedar Press, 2014

The Comedic Applicant, Blue Cedar Press, 2015

The Average Level of Happiness, Blue Cedar Press, 2016

Human Ink: The First Five Books, Blue Cedar Press, 2017

Ain't Leavin' This House Rough-Dried, Spartan Press, 2019

An Incident That Might Lead To Something,
Spartan Press, 2020

You Must Have Your Famine, Spartan Press, 2021

Lies I've Heard or Told

Poems by Michael Poage

Spartan
Press

Spartan Press

Kansas City, MO

spartanpress.co

Spartan
Press

Many thanks to the following publishers, my deepest gratitude for their support and publication of my previous books: Black Stone Press, Woodley Press, Penthe Press, 219 Press, Blue Cedar Press, Spartan Press.

A special thank you and note of deep gratitude to my wife, the scholar, activist, professor, and writer, Dr. Gretchen C. Eick who writes powerful, ground-breaking prose with the heart and touch of a poet...and, as in many cases, does not receive the praise and affirmation she deserves.

TABLE OF CONTENTS

Dedicated to my sister, Mary Ann Verrow,
for her courage, kindness, strength, open mind,
and her love.

"But God bless the child that's got his own,
that's got his own."

- Holiday and Herzog

Lies I've Heard or Told

DOWN, CHILD

This is not
the usual syndrome.
The medical professionals
have tracked the heart
to a small canyon
in a small country
just below the mountains.
The down, child
apparently tries to
quiet the heart's beating
as it grieves the world's beating.

LIES I'VE HEARD OR TOLD

I love you.

I hate you.

We are now out of Iraq.

There are WMDs in Iraq so we must invade.

No, there isn't someone else.

Yes, you get the children as often as I do.

We've landed on the moon.

Algebra is easy.

I was at the library studying.

You're making this into something it's not.

You have beautiful legs.

I don't miss my dead parents.

You look twenty years younger than that.

You look ten years younger than him.

You look great!

The bottled water is better for you than tap.

I feel great!

Every joint in my body hearts.

Yes, you get the children as often as I do.

Trust me.

STAGE FOUR

A scowl of sand
forms a mask covering your
face like an ancient desert god
or a tomb. The labor of so many
works the already dangerous tiny warriors
into an army many nations
try to defeat. 'I thought maybe an ulcer,'
says one. 'I guessed it was just allergies,'
from another. Fools. They tried a wet cloth
at the bottom of the door, tape around
the windows, a lifeline from the backdoor
to the barn. Nothing worked, nothing could kill
the forecast as it metastasized into a scowl of dust.

SANDEND

On her walk to Sandend
she helped herself to the
ripening blackberries even
bringing some home in her
stained hands. The berries
were large and juicy, the stains
hard to remove. She realized
the juice had made its mark
all the way around her body,
the skin becoming its own
blackberry flesh. This only happens
on the dirt pathway to Sandend
where passion runs deep above
the sea and human life comes
so close to the sweet salt of love.

SYRIA

I speak respectfully of my broad shoulders
made fun of since I was a young girl
playing in the dusty streets near my home.

I speak of how I prefer to be cold rather
than bundled up in some bulky coat
keeping my arms bound and useless.

Did I mention how I sing with the beautiful
storms? How I love the thunder, the large
dark clouds, slashes of vibrant lightening?

But I speak mostly of my love for the rain.
And I tell my family in Damascus of these
Kansas storms, so different from my home.

When I play my violin, I am moved, not
to tears, but to exhaustion. The dread
of the distance forces the blood from my
fingers. They are grey like Aleppo and my lips.

PANSION STARI GRAD

Juliet, Juliet, that is the hurting part.
You wake up
and in the mirror
see your life
only
in black and white.
Juliet, that is the hurting part.
It's a life-threatening situation for those of you
living north of Paradise, praying in Nebraska. Juliet
open your eyes
as you wake up
see yourself
in black and white.
Your life
depends on it, north of Paradise, the hurting part.
Juliet, Juliet,
and it's grown to be
a life-threatening situation for
those of you under siege in Stari Grad, across the ocean
from Paradise, that is the hurting part,
open your eyes, see the blackbirds, thirteen
of them only in black and black
you wake up.
Your life depends
on it, the situation
threatening Paradise,
Juliet, Juliet, you are
not invited to the party, open your eyes to the life-
threatening possibilities north of Paradise.
Juliet, Juliet, that is the hurting part.

HESTER'S SITUATION

Few could see the wild child
and not think devil, demon.
Hester had a rough job, not only
to care for her little Pearl and fight
to keep her but also to carry on her breast
the "A" with golden thread skillfully
wrought with a flourish
or two or three that bravely brought eyes
to the letter (or the breasts) returning
an "up yours" to all the Boston divines.

THE FRIGATE BIRD

I look forward to Ira on NPR's Science Friday
each week. Not that I know much about science
or even remember his subjects or guests. But even
the video streaming specialist, a young woman, is so excited
about the subject of the week whether it's a frigate bird or an
almost extinct spider. They are both so happy, it's in their voices,
about the next story or the scientist who talks about the Rover's
footprints or beautiful neon algae so deep in the sea. My spirit
is lifted out of Gaza City or Baton Rouge for a few
moments, not long, but a few childlike seconds that soon
turn me back to a world that spits out hope
like the blood and teeth of the boxer who lost.

EGYPTAIR 804

We turned hard to the left
then spun in the opposite
direction like a drunk laboring
to make up his mind. In slow
tortured motion
pieces of us fell away into space.
There went my husband and my heart
torn out of my chest
still pounding.
I stopped breathing long before we
hit the sea but I am sure I heard someone
scream about a god
as I joined the drowning dead
scratching our beautiful hieroglyphic drawings
drifting along as we did
so centuries from now professional or amateur
archeologists would attempt to translate our story, a
miraculous find, on the sandy floor of the sea.

HEAVEN

Sometimes I think that in heaven
given there is one, those of us who need it
will be allowed to finally break open the dam
and cry as much as we want, for as long
as we want. I envision it as similar to last
February 5th when I had to put down my fourteen
year old dog. He was on a stretcher on the floor
of the vet's exam room. He had been given
something to relax him, ease the pain, I put my forehead
gently on his head and had my hands under his jaw
gently on his head and had my hands under his jaw
trying to comfort him and I just sobbed and sobbed as he died
and for as long as I felt I could in front of those
few people. Heaven, perhaps, will not impose such
limits. And if you need to laugh and laugh you are welcomed.
Or maybe simply rest in silence, sleep for a hundred years.

A WORD HERE

Let's do this small
lyric together. You
think of one word:
_____. Good,
Now I will add,
"throat." Your next
word is: _____.
So, I will add, "tree."
And we will go back
and forth like that until
we make a new thing,
and we will have a gift
for each other, we will
stop fighting, everyone
will stop yelling and
shooting and dropping
cluster bombs and using
chemical weapons. We
will share this gift of
gentle words, of poetry
and peace with each
of you gathered around
the world, even just one,
especially even just one.

Five hard pieces

of rain
played their music
in concert on my gutter
tonight

        But lonely under the bridge
        spit and shake for the sake of shit
        and their music reminds the cosmic
        whisper of its significance

alone, staying away from the draining
water coming down
the hill toward the river

        pardon the world, it speaks
        for too many people serving
        as liaison
        between the evil and not so evil

and you try to figure out the difference.

CRAWL SPACE

On your own, you found a way
for days of chance
encounters with colored things that
crawled between dark rough wood
and black soft dirt, over your
legs
and into your ears. A childhood
rhyme comes to mind
or would but by now your
tongue-stuck thoughts and fears
are years
or more beyond you. Mostly people
remember you
in passing, as in passing
the stone marker, your name,
date of birth and death.

Fresh

lavender began growing
unplanted
on its own to wash the air
where the previous fragrance
was poisoned by
some hollow-hashed thoughtless hack
from a dead generation. No blame
laid. Passion back then answered
to no one. I miss you but who will know.

LIFELINE

The ink on my hand follows
the lines and wrinkles in the skin
that some call life and love. From my
fetal position on the prairie colored couch
I don't want anyone touching me, let alone
holding my hand and reading my lines like some people
divine for water or ask how I 'really' feel. No,
please, put together your own future and leave
me out of it. But not forever
although that's what it feels like. Yesterday
I held my great grandson and knowing he likes
to watch the traffic out on the street we looked out the
window with his six-month old eyes. We watched, waited.
Nothing.

HORSE AND RIDER

You have nightmares but remember
your therapist, years ago,
said the violent ones, no she *suggested*
you think the violent ones with blood
could be thought of in a positive way
as the brilliant flow of life not
the spattered, slathering of death and pain
they seemed to be. And in her office
for that few minutes of grateful insight
it worked, you could see it. Until
the next knife-involved moment of sleep
skin-mostly-red dreams coming from
somewhere and staying for a couple of days
for you to find ways to shake them loose
like a horse, tired of its rider, slams a tree.

ANOTHER WAR

You fight these internal wars
great battlefields covered with
bodies Stephen Crane couldn't
imagine. It is all so exhausting
but defense is essential not
appeasement. You are on foot now
because she stole your horse. Why not
sit down against this tree, wipe away the ants,
stop the bleeding from your wounds, wait for help.

PRAYING GLAD TELL

I pray to stop the nightmares
the ones I can't speak of except
to you the ones I can't forget
the forest enchanted old chimney's
brief and sour test of sexual skill
blood managed by money sick with fire
rancid stew of stars to slick down my hair
felony after felony touching the quiet skin
falling falling falling for the quiet skin
I'm glad, chin in hands, I can tell you all of this.

Like the ocean

the large maple sways in rhythm
with the wind, the leaves curling
and washing the rest of us with doubt
and eternal blasts of blue and red,
sky that could be the ocean and leaves
their autumn repeat of edgy calmness
and a community falling as you watch
with joyful desolation as you say those
two words aloud sitting on the ground
under the tree, hoping with the sea.

The dog (at night before bed)

I used to have to chase the _____
up to the top of _____, fence, chain link
and follow it all along the parameter
of the yard, while the _____ balanced
on the fence top. It was dark but every
night they had this ritual until the
_____ climbed up the neighbor's higher
privacy fence and ending dog's adventure
for another night-like-no-other. Last February
my dog's pain was worse than mine, much
_____, and I had to "put him down." I'd
known him longer than anyone else in my
life, 98 years or _____. People today and dogs
need each other more than ever, even with
the grief of death, wide open brown sad eyes
at the end of such a long love affair.

DECEMBER 25, 2016

Christmas music at Terminal E
            Philadelphia airport
the world is on the move
especially the children
some with cloth
            antlers, actually
many with those head ornaments
a sign of the victories achieved
                        or the pleasing of the adults

in their lives. Some moms
        have that look boarding
        the plane
that smile of endured exhaustion
like the one with a child walking
in front of her, one infant in a front sling
and one stumbling behind stepping
            on her heels. The

mom/smile is cloth, sewn in place, plastic
teeth that will break if used
                like a glass ball
                on the tree that falls. She is trying hard
                to like flying home, to show she is

happy as a clasp of coal
or a diamond.

DIONYSIUS

I'm on his trail, the backwoods
of the pantheon of the light-footed
legends we live by. I need to let
the critical remarks against me
slide away like fish down a duck's back.
Didn't it rain? And what do you mean "if?"
It's always been "when!" Curl up on the couch
with your _____, enjoy a _____
and finally relax to the world or the underworld.

THE POET'S HOUSE

The moon flowers
interrupt the dark
bringing you back
from your senses
to the more familiar
bewilderment. You feel
comfortable in the imagined
thin gown and slippers
as you step so quietly
from room to room so
you can listen to
who has been tied down
to their beds for their
own good, the screaming
crazy Janes of Yeats,
the silent brooding John Clares
with almost twenty years of
slipping poems underneath
their doors. Sometimes it's
bedlam, Sylvia writing
two or three poems a day
sometimes silent as a nail
so Emily can secretly write
for years, adding them to the bundle,
to be found later, suddenly,
we all think, like a miracle.

CROSSING OVER

I can't do it by myself.
The current is so swift
and the rocks on the floor
slippery. Please take my
blue hand, it is that cold.
I am afraid of a fall
as the world begins to fall.

PROJECTION

The men in my life, _____
Hi, I'm dating so and so
from L.A. and I just wanted
you to know _____ and it
is important to keep the pattern's
in the open so I appreciate
your _____ but let's
not overlook our life
in healing others so it continues
to be a journey. Loving my life
and my own greatness so _____ you
and we may or may not
be falling in love. O, to have
a Kauai wife.

BOSNA DREAM #1

This thin soul as you may know
has nothing to do with this skin.
Nothing! Take a peek inside any Homeric
literary epic, just a glance, and it will
be clear, terribly transparent, just to
make the point. Then lift your eyes
toward the heavens and the stone-black
pillars of the adoration. That's when,
with the adoration word, you will
curl your fists into crimson, rage-filled
lovers, not hidden well enough as, contrary
to promise, they soon appear in the crosshairs.
I notice your breathing hesitate until
automatically and with a North Sea-like
crescendo you will find that voice
you've just discovered after centuries. And
everyone around will speak of the eternal search
for the Adriatic twenty-kilometer coastal claim
and whisper the public archetype of blood.

BOSNA DREAM #2

The dog next
door, named Wade,
is barking
at the leaves
scraping and crackling
against the chain-
link fence
separating the two
countries. It's a full
out wind from
the south, summer's
tornado path
but now, on this
last night of 2016,
we fly in the face
of all storms
keeping the door
locked to all
intrusion, we listen
for heat-seeking
weapons, Bosnian dogs,
hunting.

Carry on at 1 a.m.

until the, the black birds
with those red wings
of spring, cling to the
single strong stalk
in the marsh. It is a sign
of change for those of you
in love. Known for hope
spring actually sees more
suicides than the others.
I heard on the radio life
expectancy is down a tenth
of a year. So, carry on at
1 a.m. your skin-flint sparks.

FIRST STEP

My ten-year-old grandson
woke me up from my Sunday
afternoon nap. He
gently put his arms around
me – let me know
that dinner was ready
downstairs. Then he crawled
up on the bed himself
with his back to me
and looked out the window
at the lonely winter trees
trying to make family.
I stirred and sat on the edge
of the bed. He came over to me,
took my arm saying
let me help you, grandpa.
Outside the trees were
fighting a cold wind,
struggling to make sense
of so many changes.
When we reached the
bedroom door
my grandson let go
of my arm, smiled, and said
now, you're on your own.

HUMAN RIGHTS SABBATH-2016

Your childhood memory
is cold like an unsolved
crime, which is what the police
call a mystery remaining.
The years you've thrown
behind you come together
as a Sabbath, a rest,
a recollection on this day
of chemicals and clusters,
some choked hope in poison
dust as you collect the remains
no one you love can even hold.

SUSTAINED LAMENTATION

This is a new phrase
to me coming after a sermon
in Advent this morning.
It is December 2016, so
perhaps those two words
are a gift for this time,
this country. We are in
a national emergency and
a spiritual desperation both
leading to some of us,
some of you, anxious for a
direction or method of
sustaining lament. Remember
brokenness and wholeness are
not opposites but two sides
of the same coin, so use caution
when tossing that coin into the
air, let it drop to the ground
without inference. We could all
join the rich, be sent empty away.

COHEN'S ALLELUIA

You are trying to work your way
into a better space. Listen
to life and its songs, to death
and its whispers, to finding and
to searching: Why that punctuation
behind you? God could pound
all over this savage yard, salvage
yard and make no discoveries worth
your thin-skulled syndrome. Take
your day in mortal slathering
as an example. Dig the plow deep
into the blackened earth, hoping for some
god-shed to crawl into and your
storm-force, snow-packed face sings
the small "a" alleluia off the tongue.

BOY IN THE BOOK

The daydark is here
much sooner than expected
along with the custodial
tasks of bucket
and soap, broom and
old rag to wipe the Scottish
slate. I start at the far
end of the sacred
floor and walls and roof
and move, often on my knees,
merely removing the grime
from the toenails of clerical
misbehavior and hard sleep,
sweat curling among the hairs
of life, liberation,
libation. Last night, sitting
on the couch, watching a TV movie,
I sat alone surrounded
by the flesh and burn
of family present and loathing
and faces of abduction and
desertion, rage and smiles
just to make it the whole time
I remained on the couch
in the midst of the silence
of disbelief along with
the rag to wipe it all away.

DIVINE COMEDY

You have
a sense of humor
like the ornate
box turtle
our state
reptile. But,
I am told,
it's all in
the timing.
So,
I wait.

TIME TRAVELING

The slow station
rolled gently into view
as those departing
stood in the aisle
with coats and quiet
gladness fear and
who can tell
what else. Others
boarded with eyes
forward hoping for
a seat to themselves
because most of us
like it that way
because, well,
who can tell.

LOST AT SEA

Swales and sea gulls above
The day-dried sand that stings
Your face, while your pale skin
Flushed to pink by the cold

Dies and is gone forever except
Today. You could hold the hand
Of any lover with the same
Pale effort, indiscriminant and old.

STRANGLES

It's highly contagious
and you don't
want it. Wear the
rubber boots
and surgical
gloves when treating
the horse. The night
visions may return,
the unkind ones. Almost
deadly to your way
of thinking and your
nerve
damage. Maybe
it's the same as
removing two day old
dead lambs in utero
with a scalpel,
hope you don't
have on your hand
or near your throat
an open wound.

QUAKER MIDNIGHT

Sunday
she says
is very hard

and, yes, for
some reason, I
reply, it's been

the saddest day
of the week all
my life. Has

she heard from
her love, I ask. That's
most of the trouble,

her loneliness,
confusion. She mentions
church, that it helped

a little. I reply
but can't remember
what I said - about

church - I feel
nauseous from the
chemo. I roll over,

stop thinking about
the pain, start thinking
about the pain

around us, close my eyes
no later than ten or
around Quaker midnight.

Try carrying the other's

burden for just
a short time. You
can see the light
of strict kindness
like a hit and run
accident sending
the victim into the air
fighting for life,
touching the stars
and sweeping the
highway with
the long arms
of singular strife.
Carry the other's burden
like a hit and run
fighting for life,
the long arms
touching the stars
of singular strife
like a hit and run
fighting for life.

THE GOSPEL GOODS

There was no snow today
And it didn't even rhyme.
You forced semi-articulate words
From your vocal appetite in time

For local residents to hear
The loud, street-corner sermon fake
A word-of-god praise from horse-
Induced ecstasy and you will take

The final devil, cleanse it
From me as the grit and grime
Of nights driveling in lost houses
Burns and burns from Jesus' crime.

There was

rain today,
the kind of slow soaking
dark rain that makes a break
with the light of day
allowing the ground to drink
and eyes to open gently
to the horizon and black earth.
Graveyards across the high prairie
surrounded by barbed wire
find consolation on days like this.

THE TRAINS

It's about the same as
every night. The trains
moving north through
the bedroom window
and out the bathroom
with a much smaller window.
I've tried since I was a kid
to figure out how that happened
but this is a magic land
with love and loss, seventy year
marriages, then a massive stroke,
hospice and in two short weeks' time
a burial on the prairie.
So much magic. Just ask one of the
train conductors or anyone
traveling the yellow brick road.

The nightlight

throws shadows against the wall
like an abuser,
like a slob dishing it out
against his only son.
The nightlight is placed in your room
to give you comfort, but you know
it's true, not-so-clandestine, purpose.

FALL TO WINTER

I thought of your hand
reaching across the café table
touching my arm so kindly.
Do you remember the sky
we watched? The strong clouds
and the birds flying into the fearful
unknown, escaping one season
for another? They moved
using careful instinct, with a connection
I still, I still wish for us
to escape one season for another.

THE CAIRN

The heart coiled and died
like a hot red pepper
dried up and discarded in the garden.
Don't touch me, it said, I am not ready.
The birds came only so close because they understood.
Gradually, other dead things gathered around
the heart as they were discarded
and dried up as well. 'O my god,
I'm crawling out of my skin,' was over-heard
from under the cairn. The gathering grew. The day
faded into dark, our brothers and sisters
came to the memorial for the dried up and discarded.
It has since been used as a marker for our path
into the dreams, centuries ahead, toxic playing fields
seen through thought-dead shadows cast by the moon
shining on the pile of coiled hearts and dry.

THE QUARRY

The abandoned quarry was our
community swimming pool. It had
just enough water from rain and runoff
for us to wade out in our underwear
and swim but still be able to touch the bottom
with our feet. It was, as you would expect,
a test of bravery among the several boys
choosing to disobey our parents' warning. On hot
summer days we would walk through the Maine woods
to the water-filled rock quarry, strip-down and splash into
our own private pool. I was the youngest therefore
also a target for the oldest one. As I stood ankle-deep in the
water he came up behind me, put one hand on the back of
my neck and the other down my underpants. As he felt around,
my feet sunk deeper into the shallow mud. I was stuck and
would see myself as the youngest for the rest of my life.
When he finished, I sat down in the water, balancing
myself with my two hands. My right hand immediately
became numb and pulling it into the air, I saw a deep cut
from broken glass just below the surface. The blood mixed
with the mud and the water. Tonight I see that scar as I
write, write this poem. Every night I write poems
to try to heal the scars but so often I just tear off the scab.

PLEASURE

'Keep awake,' I kept telling myself
All night. The street was too quiet,
Maybe it was the rain. Or the chill
In the air. No one telling some casual
Lie to leave the apartment. No one so
Lonely that it's not even worth the
Simplest of pleasures. Here comes a car
Moving slowly, first one in an hour.
It closes in on the curb, I take a
Step, barely out of the shadows.
"You pervert," he yells and throws a
Beer bottle at me. It breaks on the sidewalk
Behind me. The car speeds away and I quickly
Move back against the abandoned building.
The dark is sucking the life out of me instead
Of the other way around. It is still raining.
I'm shaking a little more and it's not the air.

GRASSROOTS

I spent the afternoon making calls
for the Democratic Party in my Kansas
county. Mostly to older patriots
using Advance Voting ballots, making
sure, they had received their ballots from
the county clerk. I'm very fearful of
"massive voter fraud." Isn't everyone?
A lot of people weren't home on Saturday
so, I left many recorded messages. I had a
long conversation with Ora, age 91.
"I've seen a lot of elections and this
is the craziest one of all." I agreed
and asked her if she had more
questions of me. Ora said, "No,
but I've got a lot of questions for the idiot
Republicans, like our governor." She
went on, Ora at 91. "My mother-in-law,
she's dead now so I can say this, was
such a blind-headed Republican that she'd
vote for a retarded snail if it was her party."
I ignored her politically incorrect language,
she's 91, we're in Kansas, and she's a Democrat.

LEARNING TO SPEAK

You've been crying a lot recently
at the sparrows and cardinals feeding
on the other side of the large window
in the kitchen. The clouds disturb
whatever happiness your life started with
in the morning. "A warm human plumpness
settled down on his brain" (Joyce's *Ulysses*).
There's the sentence that tells us all how
you feel having to wait out the oral decay
of aphasia and the hard work of recovery.
You're crying a lot, phoneme, by word, by god.

Tomorrow is a tight fit

although another poet wrote
it would be a "tight fist." For you
the truth belongs
against the black boulders like fat soldiers
in a children's story or rhyme.
They are never as simple as our
simple desires make them with ghosts,
lions and two or three syllable words
at the most. When you or I pay attention
as we watch the rock-bashing sea
we will also watch the children's difficult days
then our own dawn emerges tight as a fit can get.

THE LIGHTENING LAB

Was it murder? Or simply
a push at the top of the stairs
soul's hands clapping
breathing stopped
without the breaking of the neck
negatively charged attracted to the
positive and here in the lab
for lightening before and after a normal
lunch and we all are normal for the sake
of all experiments left for us in this lifetime.

THE CLEAN FIELD

After being harvested and harrowed
your neighbor's sheep and goats wander
the clean field. The rain falling
now will soon cause the loose
grains to sprout and the stock
will graze slowly, almost like
statues or toys from far away
along the fence line next to the sea.
Then the rocks you see like gray
steel beams angled and thrusting
seismic power from the gravel, sand
and seaweed. Gazing toward Arctic
waters you must watch as you
stumble, tremble with the thought
that the same Arctic still sends air
to you cold enough for your haunted
bones to empty their marrow-life deep
and forever to be ice-bound and waiting.

IT'S A HARD LIFE

In 1670 the harbor was begun,
finished fourteen years later, first
on the Morayshire coast. You walk near
the sea wall in your stubborn
stone-hacked way. The loves you carried
on your scrubbed shoulders betray
the salt lips of the drowned and those
who ran to the inland forest of the
fishwives, flesh wives, early to die.

WRITING IN SCOTLAND

The sea from the north rises
in a storm-rush against the ancient madness
of rock and sin. Daylight of the morning
frightened by the deadly dive of birds
bright that day of all the years
loved and dissolved, using the "f" word
in graceful conversations to end
all intercourse. At least spell the words
correctly and give us a clear view
as you stretch your arm around her shoulders,
those smooth olive-touched, that unable-to-describe
body of work labeled and labored into your life.

CROSSING THE IRISH SEA

"The way up
and the way down
are one." --Heraclitus

This is one of those
turboprop
planes with the wing above
the fuselage so you feel
like you are hanging by a thread –
shades of Jonathan Edwards and the angry God –
above the sea
and if you sin, SNAP,
you fall
something like 19,000 feet
all drowned out
before you hit
the water. But this flight is pure,
without sin, quiet, for the moment
until the clouds
reflecting the wet morning light
hide from sight
the runway.

THE COST OF IT ALL

The feel of this carved swimmer
making small waves keeps the heart
beating and gives my breath a catch
like a fish. You wade through
the inch-deep, fleece-like water
meeting you where the shore allows
the sea to touch your toes and other
places you won't let me near. I'm mad
at her because she's mad at me. She says
it's done. You go your own direction,
it's the way of love in your eyes.
Salted, you awaken to the grace you paid for.

LOVE IN SCOTLAND EVEN IF

it is a fake day.
Here in Scotland, we no longer
Talk constantly
About salmon or rain.
You may notice, if you visit,
That we are deeper
Than you've come
To understand.
We say thank you to the driver
As we get off the bus.
You want to go to Cullen?
I'll drive you. And even if
It is a fake day, with laundry
Drying on the line in ten minutes,
Waves only inches high so they
Can't be described as "breaking,"
I'll get your coffee and read
The news aloud to you from
Any paper we can buy.
Here in Scotland, in my family,
It's more than the waves that "break."

2 POEMS IN BODY OF EMAIL

The flesh plucked roughly away
Told the father and son finding
The two poems in the shallows
That the body had been dead

For some time. No identification
Found with either of them and no
Family to make final arrangements.
The sacred words came from a stranger.

YOUR TRAINING DOES NOT

Your training does not
Explain the way you wear
Your hair, smile or not.
And you know that mom
Has lived long enough now
To be a problem. And the plane
We took to fly to Ireland
Was the same type that crashed
Monday in Indonesia.
The evidence keeps piling up
And you refuse to stand
As a witness to your own
Ego, the self-centered, controlling
Painkiller that saves both of us
From the everyday curse we breathe.

U.S. SUBMARINE VETERANS
MEMORIAL HIGHWAY

Huck and Jim
Missed the Ohio River.
Was it the fog?
Or the strong current?
Was it Samuel Clemens
Or Mark Twain?
We find life in the strangest
Places
And death.
And how often
We are blind to the fork
In the river. Keep your feet
In your own damn stream,
Let the catfish
Skim the bottom mud
To survive.

THE LIGHT

The light
    how it makes
a lover swim
      the breaststroke

as opposed to
    the backstroke
or rejection
      by another name.

PHRASE

You watch the ice
Begin its life on the
Skeletal trees.
There is a glaze of fear
Building across your face
Stretching like a second skin
And the hospice light glows
From the barn to the county road.
Your body is not working
So well today.
Not too good
Or not too well?
"Pick the suitable phrase,"
You say, "while I use the bathroom
Again."
While you are away
The visitor, from a nearby cattle ranch,
Puffs up your pillow,
Gets you a fresh glass of water and new straw.
You return, notice the kindness,
And exchange a thank you
For the visitor's you're welcome.
You reach for the simple words
That express -- goodbye, and,
I've lived a full life.

YOUR STORY

Every story has a flip side
And a life so ingenious
That another could sweep
It away after it dies
On the sidewalk, unidentified.

A life so ingenious that another
Could sweep it away, turn
The flip side away from sight
So she could go to the city park,
She was feeling so much better.

FROZEN

-Translated by anonymous

I.

I'm a world unto myself.
Just like you
And you and all of us gathered here
At the edge of the forest
Of ice. Songs miraculously
Remembered by generations
Of the loved, the un, the lost
And the one I saw melted
The other day.

II.

Your hand is gentle along its path
On my leg. This honeymoon has begun
Long before the word was ever invented.
Now, there are so many of us to watch over,
Each angel needing two or three to carry on.

GOLDEN WEDDING ANNIVERSARY

We could not
Stand each other
For one more meal
Or television show,
Another sweet smile
Smothered in gravy
Or a traffic jam
The length of 10
From Santa Monica
To wherever it finally
Finds alleluia freedom
Which Janis Joplin
Reminds us is a
Word for nothing
Left to lose.

65.

AS I GROW OLDER

I want fifteen (for now) important items
tended to in a timely manner:

Trim my toenails
Trim my fingernails
Trim nose and ear hairs
Make sure my socks are clean
And my underwear, especially my underwear
And my glasses
I want my hair cut handsomely short and neat
    like my scotch
I want my children, grandchildren and
    great grandchildren to know I
    am alive until I am not
Find the damn democrats some GUTS
Somewhere
Ask Cora to explain "SELF AS SOULMATE"
Treat every faith and non-faith
    Community carefully, we are
    all terribly wounded
I am a "veteran of the cross" so see
    if some money can come of it
When I stop laughing
    Someone pick up where I left off
Do you have any questions?

Lies I've Heard or Told is the fourteenth collection of poems published by **Michael Poage.** He was born in Virginia but has lived and traveled across the U.S. as well as Europe, the Middle East, Egypt, and Mexico. In 1973 he earned an MFA in Creative Writing and Literature from the University of Montana, studying with Madeline DeFrees and Richard Hugo. In 2017-18, he was the Poet-in-Residence at Dzemal Bijedic University in Mostar, Bosnia and Herzegovina. During the academic year, 2021-22, he taught English literature and usage virtually at Walailak University, Thailand. He lives in Wichita, Kansas with his wife, the scholar, professor, and activist, Dr. Gretchen Eick.

This project was made possible, in part, by generous support from the Osage Arts Community.

Osage Arts Community provides temporary time, space and support for the creation of new artistic works in a retreat format, serving creative people of all kinds — visual artists, composers, poets, fiction and nonfiction writers. Located on a 152-acre farm in an isolated rural mountainside setting in Central Missouri and bordered by ¾ of a mile of the Gasconade River, OAC provides residencies to those working alone, as well as welcoming collaborative teams, offering living space and workspace in a country environment to emerging and mid-career artists. For more information, visit us at www.osageac.org

Osage Arts Community